FROM TRIGGERED TO
Transformed

JOURNEY TO
SELF-DISCOVERY AND PURPOSE

DELLA M. MAJOR

Copyright © 2022 Della Major

Scripture quotations marked "NASB" are taken from the New American Standard Bible®, Copyright © 1960, 1962, 1963, 1968, 1971, 1972, 1973, 1975, 1977, 1995 by The Lockman Foundation. Used by permission. Scriptures marked NKJV are taken from the New King James Version (NKJV): Scripture taken from the New King James Version®. Copyright© 1982 by Thomas Nelson, Inc. Used by permission. All rights reserved. Scriptures marked NIV are taken from the New International Version (NIV): Scripture taken from The Holy Bible, New International Version ®. Copyright© 1973, 1978, 1984, 2011 by Biblica, Inc.™. Used by permission of Zondervan. Scriptures marked NLT are taken from the Holy Bible, New Living Translation (NLT): Scriptures taken from the Holy Bible, New Living Translation, Copyright© 1996, 2004, 2007 by Tyndale House Foundation. Used by permission of Tyndale House Publishers, Inc., Carol Stream, Illinois 60188. All rights reserved. Used by permission. All rights reserved. No part of this document may be reproduced or transmitted in any form or by any means, electronic, mechanical, photocopying, recording, or otherwise, without prior written permission of the author.

From Triggered to Transformed
Journey to Self-Discovery and Purpose

Della M. Major
dmajor01.dm@gmail.com
info@youcanlyve.com
www.facebook.com/CoachDellaMaeMajor
www.instagram/iamdellamajor

ISBN 978-1-943342-16-7

Printed in the USA.
All rights reserved

Published by: Destined To Publish | Flossmoor, Illinois
www.DestinedToPublish.com

DEDICATION

This book is dedicated to my daughters, Marie and Brittany. You have been the wind beneath my wings! When I could not see my way, you were the sunshine that brightened my day. I love you both unconditionally for you are God's perfect melody in my love song.

Love,

Mom

ACKNOWLEDGMENTS

I thank my heavenly Father for saving me and allowing me to see another day. I am in awe of all the many blessings that He has bestowed upon me in this journey called Life. He made me His 21st century miracle on August 18, 2019, when I received my kidney transplant. I now have my second chance in life to serve Him for the rest of my days.

I am thankful to my family for supporting me throughout my personal trauma and health crisis. Thank you for your love and words of encouragement. When I thought I was not going to make it, you were right there with me. I appreciate your support in helping me to reach my new goal in life.

I am thankful for the many women of God who helped mold me, shape me, and even challenge me to press forward in this journey when things seemed to get a little tough. I appreciate your wisdom and guidance as I prepared for this task.

Acknowledgments

I am thankful to my accountability sisters: Regina, Sabrina, and Stacy. Each one of you has a special place in my heart, for God has used you to supply the missing pieces that completed the puzzle, shaping me into the Woman of God that I am today.

I would like to give special thanks to Deborah C. Anthony, my literary coach. Thank you so much for "snatching" my edges and helping me to see the value in myself. Your compassion and patience helped me to see that there is value in what I say and what I write. Thank you for being my coach and my champion.

TABLE OF CONTENTS

Introduction 1

Part One: The Journey to Self-Discovery

Chapter 1: SUID: Sudden Unexpected Impact Distress. 9
Chapter 2: Know Who You Are! 12

Part Two: Created for Greatness

Chapter 3: Words Do Hurt 18
Chapter 4: The Journey Begins. 25
Chapter 5: My Future Foretold 32
Chapter 6: A Change Brings a Change 39

Part Three: The Birth of Purpose and Identity

Chapter 7: Renew Your Mind 46

Chapter 8: Faith Walk Not Just a Faith Talk 52

Chapter 9: You Can L.Y.V.E (Living Your Life Victorious and Empowered).......... 58

Endnotes 63

INTRODUCTION

....

"God uses our brokenness to make us even more beautiful. It's the place of brokenness where God comes in to restore and renew."
–James Prescott

Kintsugi is a Japanese art technique for repairing broken pieces. In *kintsugi*, broken pottery pieces are put back together with gold. That which might have been considered beyond repair and useless is reconstructed into a piece representing something stronger, more unique, and more beautiful. Every flaw and imperfection becomes more valuable because of what is in the broken places.

The Merriam-Webster dictionary defines *abandonment* as the relinquishment, giving up, or renunciation of an interest. A synonym for the word *abandonment* is *rejection*. For most of my life, I had to deal with feelings of abandonment and rejection by my mother and father. Since

I was a child, I have always coveted a relationship with my father. I was three years old when he left Mississippi and left me and my mother behind. Year after year, I was disappointed with the lack of my father's presence in my life. Every day, my mother would say to me that my father did not love me, nor did he want me. I grew up believing that my father had abandoned and rejected me. It was after my twelfth birthday that my father came to visit me. I was so excited and happy that my father wanted to visit and spend time with me, yet he was prevented from doing so. My mother was bitter, hurt, and angry; so much so that she would not allow my father to see me or spend any time with me. As a result of my mother denying him time with me, he left and never returned. He was once again absent from my life. I felt abandoned and rejected all over again.

MY DIVORCE

> *Now to the married I command, yet not I but the Lord: A wife is not to depart from her husband. [11] But even if she does depart, let her remain unmarried or be reconciled to her husband. And a husband is not to divorce his wife.*
>
> 1 Corinthians 7:10-11 (NKJV)

I always wanted to be married. My marriage defined who I was and whom I had become. It was my identity. I finally

Introduction

belonged to someone, and I was a part of something. I was no longer alone; I was loved and accepted. I believed my marriage was the solution to overcoming the deep hurt that I experienced by the abandonment and rejection of my parents. It brought me joy. I was living my dream life: a good marriage, healthy children, and a good job—until it all came crashing down in the summer of 2007, after I became drastically ill.

I was hospitalized for seven days after being diagnosed with lupus nephritis, which caused my kidneys to enter stage 4 renal failure. My doctors explained to me that my kidneys were failing, and I would need dialysis if I was going to survive. I was broken emotionally when I received the diagnosis from my doctor, for I knew from that moment on my life would not be the same. I simply could not understand or comprehend why this was happening to me at this point of my life. My mental state became unstable. After arriving home from the hospital, when my husband did not ask about my well-being, I instantly knew something was wrong.

You can image the mental state I was in at that time, but nothing could have prepared me for what was coming next. After 15 years of marriage and at my most vulnerable and weakest state, my husband asked me for a divorce. I was shocked and very perplexed. I could not understand why he had chosen that moment to ask me for a divorce. You see, divorce symbolizes broken promises, broken dreams, and a broken identity. My marriage defined my identity as a wife, a mother, and a Christian woman. It represented who I was and whom I would become as a married Christian woman. My identity and status in society were based on being married. Going through a divorce would be another death in my life. It would be the death of my dream and my hope for a better future. I lacked identity as a child and now, as a divorced Christian woman, I lacked identity in Christ. I truly did not know who I was anymore, nor did I know whom I would become. Once again, I felt abandoned and rejected.

Knowing who you are is important in defining your identity. Self-awareness not only aids in self-identification, but it outlines how others should define you as well. Defining your identity is a self-representation of your culture, interests, relationships, and efficacy in doing the things that matter to you. It builds up your self-esteem and confidence, which are important to your overall health and well-being. Not knowing who I was as an individual caused me to end up marrying a person just like me. As a result, my marriage ended in disaster. Nevertheless, my divorce was the trigger that started me on my journey of self-discovery and defining my identity.

I am known as a "radical of heart," and I have a slogan that I live by: "A change brings a change." I personally know the reality of change. The word *transformation* means to change the outward form or appearance; to

Introduction

change in character or condition. So many people find themselves basing their self-worth and identity on what other people think and how others see them. *From Triggered to Transformed* is a narrative about my journey of self-discovery and finding my identity. This book will tell the story of my unique personal experiences of survival and overcoming abandonment and rejection in my life. It will be a testament of where God has brought me from to where God is leading me to.

The purpose of this book is to educate, inspire, and empower women who have had life-changing events that triggered their need to transform their lives from the inside out. In each chapter, I will dive deeply into topics as they relate to triggers that have had a negative or positive impact in every area of my life, specifically, my mindset, health, faith, relationships, and finances. Through sharing my story, I hope to provide you with godly wisdom and insight that will help you to create a positive change in your life so you might know who you are and discover your purpose, develop self-worth, and maximize your full potential; a life in which you are not just surviving, but thriving. A broken crayon still colors and a broken woman still has value and has something to offer the world.

PART ONE

THE JOURNEY TO SELF-DISCOVERY

CHAPTER 1

SUID: Sudden Unexpected Impact Distress

> *When you are in distress and all these things happen to you, in the latter days you will return to the Lord your God and listen to His voice.*
>
> **—Deuteronomy 4:30 (NASB)**

My sister was 11 months old when she died. The cause of her death was never determined. The coroner said her death was due to sudden unexpected infant death (SUID), which is a term used to describe the sudden and unexpected death of a baby less than one year old. These deaths often happen during sleep or in the baby's sleep area. Nobody could explain to my mother how such a thing could happen, especially at 11 months old. The grief of my sister's death affected my mother so much that it became hard for her to care for me and my sibling. I was ten years old at the time of my sister's death. Life as I knew it changed drastically. As the oldest sibling, I had to step up and take care of my family.

DEATH OF MY AMERICAN DREAM

Some say the American Dream is to grow up, get married, buy a house with a white picket fence, have children, and live happily ever after. If only that dream could have come true for me. I was a 10-year-old child with the hope of attaining the American dream, but it was not to be. It was on a hot summer day when my mother ran into my Aunt Rose's grocery store, where I was working as a stock clerk. You might not think that a child who is 10 years old would have a job, but for me, living on the west side of Chicago, it was not unusual. Working was normal, and it meant everything. I had the opportunity to make money, have some fun, and spend a whole lot of time with my family at my auntie's convenience store. Yeah, I was the 10-year-old kid just living the dream! Making money, buying all the candy that I could eat...until that one life-defining moment when my mother ran into the store and screamed, "My baby, my baby! Something is wrong with my baby!"

I went into shock; I was numb. My heart was racing so fast that I could hear every heartbeat. It was as if my

SUID: Sudden Unexpected Impact Distress

heart had come out of my chest. I did not know what was happening; in that moment, everything was chaos. I watched my Aunt Rose kneeling in front of my mother, who was shaking and rocking back and forth right in the open doorway in front of the store. In dismay, I ran across the street to our house and up the 11 stairs to my mother's bedroom. As I opened the door, I felt a chill come over my body as I looked toward my mother's bed. That is where I saw my sister lying face down and looking lifeless. She was not moving or kicking her feet like I had always seen her do before. Afraid, I started to move towards the bed where she lay. I reached out to touch her hand, calling out her name, *Felicia*. Her touch was cold, and her skin looked blue. I had never seen anything like that before.

I knew something was wrong, for when I touched her, she was cold as ice. The EMT ran into the room and moved me out of the way. He picked her up, turned her over and patted her on the back, and that is when I saw the blood clot fall onto the bed. Not understanding what was happening, I saw him turn and look at my mother and tell her that she was dead. I instantly felt a deep sharp pain in the pit of my stomach, and I knew my life was about to change. My American dream was gone! Why? Because my mother, in her grief, turned to me and said, "You killed my baby!" Yes, my mother accused me of my sister's death. It was a *sudden unexpected impact distress* that changed my life.

CHAPTER 2

Know Who You Are!

Before I formed you in the womb I knew you, before you were born I set you apart; I appointed you as a prophet to the nations
—**Jeremiah 1:5 (NIV)**

For years, I felt abandoned by my mother. She gave up on caring for us, her remaining living children. Following my sister's death, the responsibilities that were placed on my shoulders were very heavy, for my mother had to stop working and go on welfare. In her grief, my mother turned to drinking heavily, so I had to help care for my sisters and brothers. It was hard trying to go to school, do homework, and make sure that there was food on the table.

There were many times that I blamed myself for everything that was happening. I believed that my life had no meaning and that I was a mistake. I would say to myself, *I wish I had never been born.* The pain of rejection ran deep into my soul. My mother resented my father for leaving us when I was three years old. Every day, I would hear how much she hated him for it and how my father did not love me. I had no purpose, and I had no identity. I believed that both my mother and my father had rejected me.

FROM HIS EYES TO MY EYES

Psalm 27:10 (NIV) states, *"Though my father and mother forsake me, the Lord will receive me."* This verse was my sense of hope and strength; it let me know that I was not a mistake. I was created for greatness and created to bring change. Life has not been easy for me; in fact, life has been crazy. However, the bigger picture is that I was born with a purpose. God already knew the journey that I would have to take to get to my destiny and purpose. You see, God will not place more on you than you can bear! It was God's will to allow this journey in my life. Why? Because He knew I could handle it.

Knowing who you are and whose you are gives you the knowledge and kingdom authority to overcome each and every obstacle that tries to distract you or hinder you from moving forward. I believed that my identity was what other people said it was. I did not see my own value or self-worth. If I had had just one person to validate me, that would have been enough. I had never known real love before, so I thought I was not deserving of it. I relied upon acceptance and false love from other people. I coveted it from my mother, my father, my children, my husband, and my friends, but I always felt a void on the inside. I felt empty and I simply could not understand why…until I started to see myself through God's eyes. Through God eyes, I saw that God loved me with an *agape* love! Psalm 139:14 (NIV) says that "***I am beautifully and wonderfully made.***" Everything about me was created and molded to perfection by God himself.

I began to see that the love that God had for me I didn't have for myself. The reason for the deep void on in the inside was that I didn't love myself. I did not know who I was! I began to think to myself, *How can I love and serve other people if I cannot love and serve myself first?*

If I was to be transformed into all that God has intended for me to become and discover my identity, I was going to have to learn to become my own best friend. I had to see the value in myself first before I could see the value in others.

My journey of self-discovery was learning to love myself first. My journey to transformation began with a changed mindset. I had to learn to change the way I thought, and to come to see myself as a woman of worth. I had to learn that no matter what someone else thought about me, it was what I thought about myself that mattered. Psalm 139:13-16 (NIV) says, "*For you created my inmost being; you knit me together in my mother's womb.* [14] *I praise you because I am fearfully and wonderfully made; your works are wonderful; I know that full well.* [15] *My frame was not hidden from you when I was made in the secret place, when I was woven together in the depths of the earth.* [16] *Your eyes saw my unformed body; all the days ordained for me were written in your book before one of them came to be.*"

My journey began with seeing myself how God sees me. Everything about me was written in God's book of life before I came into existence. My purpose was already formed, and my destiny was already set. It was up to me to embrace my purpose and my destiny. It was up to me to know who I am and whose I am.

My divorce was the trigger for me to see that had I placed my identity and my purpose in other people's hands. I believed I had been validated and had overcome my childhood hardship when I became a married woman. My focus was not on my problems or my hurt from the past; it was living in the present with my family. So, when my marriage ended, I felt lost, abandoned, and rejected all over again. I spent half of my life living a lie for other people. I did not truly know who I was nor what I wanted for myself. There is a saying that I quote all the time: "A half of a woman and a half of a man does not make a whole marriage or person." You must know who you are first. You must be willing to be made whole! It is only then that you will be able to move forward towards next-level living.

Here are 4 steps to accepting yourself as God sees you:

1. Know that all your flaws and imperfections were created by God.
2. Speak daily affirmations:
    a. I am beautiful
    b. I am strong
    c. I was created for greatness
    d. I was created to have dominion and subdue all that God has created
    e. I am the beloved of God
    f. I am a child of the King of Kings
    g. I am co-heir with Jesus Christ
    h. I have a regulated and sound mind
3. Think daily on things that are lovely, pure, and of good report
4. Believe in yourself

PART TWO

CREATED FOR GREATNESS

CHAPTER 3

Words Do Hurt

"Sticks and Stones can break my bones, but words CAN really hurt me!"

—*Anonymous*

For many years, I was teased often by my family and friends. My reply would always be, "Sticks and stones may break my bones, but words will never hurt me." As an adult, I found that the old adage was no longer true. The truth is that words do hurt. Certain words can heal you while others can hurt or destroy you. Although words cannot physically harm you, they often are used as triggers that cause emotional and physical scars.

The Bible says in Proverbs 18:21 (NKJV): *"Death and life is in the power of tongue, and those who love it will eat its fruits."* Hurtful words can trigger something in the brain that can cause pain in your heart or your inner being even before that pain is ever felt. Medical researchers have found that words such as "excruciating" or "grueling" can activate the area in your brain that sends the signals that cause painful sensations in your body.

Harsh or hurtful words uttered by a trusted adult such as a parent, teacher, or favorite relative can hit a child as hard as a fist to the stomach. Although no bones are broken, those words can leave a vicious emotional scar. Inflicted repeatedly for years, those words can shatter a child's self-image, self-esteem, and identity, turning that child into a bitter, angry, and lost adult.

For most of my adult life, my mother would say hurtful things to me like, "You are not going to amount to anything in life," "Your father did not love you," or "He did not want anything to do with you." She would say, "I wish you were never born" or "I brought you into this world, I can take you out." Year after year, I would simply internalize her words, which left internal emotional scars that ran deep down into my inner soul. Her words I would hold deep down within my heart.

CYCLE OF SORROW AND NO SELF-WORTH

The heart is the epicenter of our soul. It is that secret place where we reason, question, meditate, think, and motivate. It is our soul that contains our mind, our will, and our emotions. Hurtful words spoken at you make things very personal. When they are spoken by a loved one, they go deeper and begin to take deeper root, which causes a deeper pain within the inner soul. When hurtful words reach our soul, they can be transformed into hurtful actions. When you are deeply hurt by a loved one, you become broken mentally, emotionally, and spiritually.

The emotional scars that I received from my mother's hurtful words eventually turned into physical scars as well. The physical and emotional scars that I experienced lasted for most of my teenage years. Every day I would ask myself, *If nobody loves me, why was I ever born?* or *Why am I still here?* The hurtful words spoken to me by my mother and the emotional and physical pain that I experienced took root so deep in my heart and my soul that one day, I decided to get rid of the pain. On a late summer evening in June of 1980, I attempted suicide. Although I survived, my inner pain did not go away. As a matter of fact, it became worse. Yes, I was alive, and the pain that I felt lived on!

For years, I kept up a facade that everything was okay in my life. On the surface, people would see me laughing and smiling all the time. I gave the appearance of being a strong and confident woman. But the truth was I was broken on the inside. My heart was filled with cracks from the inner pain I was experiencing from feeling rejected and abandoned and from my lack of love, low self-esteem, and lack of self-worth. The hurtful words that I held in my heart were like a small chip on a car window shield that expanded to a large, irreparable crack. The loss of intimate relationships, church family members, and friends following my divorce was the breaking point that shattered my inner being. It was the inner hurt that was too hard to bear. I had worked hard to create a life in which I had begun to feel loved, safe, and secure, and it was gone.

WHAT DOESN'T KILL YOU MAKES YOU STRONGER!

On the inside, I carried the feeling of never being "good enough" or "wanted." My heart was full of heartbreak, bitterness, sadness, and unforgiveness. I clung to the feeling of needing to belong to something or someone. That need had me constantly seeking validation from people and outside influences.

Harmful words can tear down a person's self-esteem in an instant. The words spoken to me by my mother shaped the negative image and self-worth I had about myself that damaged my life for years. I felt I did not receive the love or support that a child should have received from a parent. I was terribly hurt and emotionally scarred.

Harmful words hold the power to knock us down and derail our minds towards toxic thinking that sets and simmers within us for a very long time. Hurtful words can cause us to become angry and react in a way we might not want. It can be very hard to move past the pain, but it is possible with faith in God and applying His word in our lives. Proverbs 12:18 says, "***Some people make cutting remarks, but the words of the wise bring healing***" (NLT).

People who choose to use harmful words and put-downs are likely dealing with their own insecurities and their own inner pain and failures. Ask yourself a question: How many times have you said something negative about someone or said something harmful to someone else to make yourself look better in front of other people or to feel better about yourself? It is easy to do.

Nathan Bransford made the statement, "Words only have power if you let them." For years, my dreams of success were determined by others' opinions or thoughts about me. If they said that I was a failure, I believed that I was a failure. If they said that I was a success, then I believed that I was a success. My identity was formed by the opinions and thoughts of others. My focus was to please other people and not myself. I felt unworthy of being blessed.

The key to moving past hurtful words and living your life is learning to forgive. I learned to develop a mindset like Japanese *kintsugi* artists, who believe that broken places in your life can make you stronger and better than ever before. When you are broken, you can pick up the pieces, put them back together, and learn to embrace your brokenness. Allowing yourself to feel the hurt and grieve, you learn to accept the person you have become, and you learn to forgive, looking beyond the hurtful words and exercising compassion toward those who hurt you. For me, I had to learn how to forgive my mother, my father, and my ex-husband. No longer did I allow the pain of feeling angry, rejected, and worthless keep me from moving forward in my life. I learned to accept my flaws and my imperfections.

I embraced my cracks and defined who I was going to become moving forward. Here are five steps to help you put into practice to begin your journey of inner healing:

1. Be kind to yourself. Begin to practice self-love. Accepting your cracks means accepting and loving the person who you are. You must forgive yourself first before you can forgive others. Don't look at your brokenness as something bad; look for the beauty that shines through because of it.

2. Own your truth. True healing and self-discovery can only come when you accept your past hurts and failures. My life was centered around a marriage that failed, and I could not accept the end results. Nevertheless, for me to move forward in my self-discovery and develop my identity, I had to accept the truth that my divorce was over, and I had to

deal with the inner pain caused by my past and my present.

3. Promote a positive and changed mindset.
4. Set expectations for work that you desire to see God do in your heart. Have a heart-to-heart conversation with yourself about the deep hurt that you experienced from your past.
5. Speak healing words over yourself. Speak daily affirmations that will reframe the way you see yourself and think about yourself.

CHAPTER 4

The Journey Begins

"I am learning to trust the journey even when I do not understand it."

—*Mila Bronit*

Life is not easy! It is hard, and it is not fair. There are times in your life when you do not understand why you go through the many storms and crises that you experience. You try to figure it out, but to no avail. That is what was happening to me. I did not understand why so many things were happening to me at such a young age. I would cry out to God night after night, "Why me?" I wanted to know what I had done so wrong that I had to go through all the things that I went through. I would say to myself that I was a good person, and I did good things instead of bad, unlike my friends. I was the one who obeyed, and I only wanted to be loved. I would say to myself many times, "Why didn't my mother and my father love me? What did I do so wrong to not be loved like a child should be loved?" Time and time again, there was no answer.

When I got married, I thought I had found the love that I was seeking all my life. When I had children, I thought I would give my children all the love I had never gotten, for they were my children and the seed from my womb. Little did I know, I was totally wrong. I realized that unless you love yourself first, you cannot give or express that love towards someone else. I had been a loner child. Although I had friends, I was alone most of the time. My mother would not allow me to spend time with my friends or be away from the home long enough to have fun with them. My job was to help and support her in raising my sisters and brothers. I was the babysitter, I was the caregiver, and I was the support.

As I became an adult, that same mindset and spirit were very present in my life. I did not know how to interact with other people. I would do specific tasks if asked or needed but I was not the person who was open to spending time with other people outside of my children. Although spending time with my children brought me happiness, the joy quickly became short-lived. That same disconnected and empty feeling that I felt from my mother was still buried deep down inside of me. That is when I realized that I had to seek out an understanding of what it means to love yourself.

My journey to self-discovery and identity could not begin before I committed to look to myself first. Self-examination and refusing to place blame were key in taking control of my life. I learned I can experience real love and growth if I simply look beyond my circumstances and learn to forgive others as well as myself. Casting the blame on external factors only hinders me from moving forward in my journey of becoming all that I was created to be. My parents never taught me about value or love, nor did they teach me how to find it. It was only when I had a personal encounter with God that I experienced what true love was all about.

SALVATION AND THE CHURCH

I was 14 years old when I started going to the Kingdom Hall with my Aunt Rose. I saw this as an opportunity to get away from the house and away from my mother. The idea of going to church had never crossed my mind, nor did I have any expectations; however, I was excited to be going. At first glance, I noticed that all the children were escorted to the lower level of the building and the adults were entering a large room on the main level. Because I was new to the place, I wanted to stay with my aunt, but I was prohibited from doing so.

The Journey Begins

The atmosphere in the room was dry and dull. Although I was at church, I had expected to have some fun, but instead we were taught lessons from a booklet called the *Watchtower*. The lessons were designed to teach us how to obey our parents and behave in a good, godly manner. All during the teaching, my mind was counting the minutes until we would leave. None of the kids that I was with acted like my friends. We were a loud and lively group of teenagers. None of the teenagers that I met reflected the character that I was used to. I was bored and I couldn't wait to leave this church. Then one day my friend, who lived next door to me, asked me to attend her church with her. I was not very excited about going to church because of my experience at the Kingdom Hall, but because she was my best friend I decided to go.

Upon arriving at her church, I could feel that this experience was going to be different. I could smell the breakfast from the outside before we entered the church building. The inside of the church was small, but intimate. It had 20 long pews on both sides of the room. It had three tall stained-glass windows on both sides of the building. In the front was the pulpit, where the pastor would talk to the people. Downstairs was the basement, where the people fellowshipped each Sunday after church. Before the Sunday service, the mothers of the church prepared breakfast for the pastor and the children who arrived early. I was so excited. I had a good Southern-cooked breakfast before the service started. Once everything was over, they transitioned the room into a classroom for the children. All the teenagers were allowed to attend the church service with the adults. That really made me feel like I was part of a family.

The first impression was everything to me. After the fun and the joy I had at her church, I wanted to go again the following week. Eventually, I would join and become a member of One-Way Missionary Baptist Church. I attended church services at One Way until I was 17 years old. The relationship between my mother and me became so toxic and intense that I decided to leave and find my own place to stay. I sought help from the church, but I was turned away and told to go back home. Once again, I felt betrayed and rejected, but this time it was not by my mother; it was by the church. This was the one place I believed that I would receive help, hope, and healing, but instead I received rejection. So I turned away from the church and from God. I decided I was going to find my own way without any help from anybody. I joined a gang and started to run the streets. I would victimize individuals who appeared weak, and I would lie to get whatever I needed and wanted.

For years, I lived my life carefree and careless. I was not concerned about anything or anybody. I was on my own and I was grown. In 1986, I became pregnant with my first child. I was in a toxic relationship with my baby's father that resembled my relationship with my mother. I had hoped that we would marry once our daughter was born, but instead, my baby and I were rejected and abandoned. I was forced to raise my daughter on my own. The same cycle of abandonment and rejection would once again manifest not only in my life but now in my newborn child's as well. In October 1990, I became pregnant with my second daughter. The idea of having two daughters out of wedlock, with neither father present and active in their lives, was devastating. I started to feel the emptiness, the rejection, and abandonment all over again. I had no sense of purpose or direction. I did not know what to do or where to go anymore. I was lost.

In 1995, at 3 am on a Friday morning, my inability to trust spurred me to leave my apartment to go and spy on a male companion with whom I was in a relationship. My children were sleeping in their room, and I had convinced myself that they would be safe and that I would be back very soon. As I proceeded to leave, I felt a deep sense of warning that stopped me. I was tired of the pain, and I was tired of feeling hurt. I wanted peace, and I wanted rest. I wanted to feel happiness in my life once and for all. The weight of my feelings was so heavy that I proceeded to fall down on the floor, crying out to God for help. In my spirit, I heard a still small voice say, "Try me and I will give you rest." I felt an unction to get up off the floor and take my comforter and wrap it around me. Instantly, I fell asleep.

When I awoke the next day, I felt a peace and a change. In my spirit, I knew that my life would not be the same from that moment on. On Sunday, I had the desire to go back to One Way. For the first time in a long time, I had the desire to hear the pastor preach. On the following Sunday, I rededicated my life to Christ, and I decided to serve God. I wanted to provide my children the opportunity to be raised in an environment where real love existed and family would be truly represented. I knew I had to repair my relationships, first with God and then with my church family. All I knew was that doing so would be the beginning of my journey towards my true purpose and destiny in life.

CHAPTER 5

My Future Foretold

"For I know the plans I have for you," says the Lord. "They are plans for good and not for disaster, to give you a future and a hope."
—Jeremiah 29:11 (NLT)

I was 30 years old when I truly gave my life to Christ. I wanted to live the life that I read about in the Bible. I was in pursuit of that abundant life as described in John 10:10. I knew that in life there will be ups and downs, but nothing can prepare us for the storms that we will face. I had experienced many storms in my life and there were many times I did not know how I was going to weather those storms, but I believed that my faith in God and His word was going to see me through them.

THE SIFTING SEASON

In May 2004, I had a dream in which I heard the Spirit of the Lord speak these words to me: *"Della, Della, Satan has asked to sift you as wheat, but I have prayed for you that your faith may not fail, and when you have recovered and turned back to me again, strengthen your brothers."* These same words were spoken by Jesus to Simon Peter in Luke 22:31-32 (NLT). The phrase "sift you as wheat" is a metaphor for breaking a person down to their lowest point where they want to give up and die or simply walk away. While partaking in the Last Supper, Jesus had warned Peter that a test of his faith was coming. It was Satan's goal to crush and destroy Peter's faith to the point beyond repair. Like Peter, I had come to a point in my life where I was at a crossroad. I had arrived at the moment where my faith would be tested, and I had to decide to whether I was going to give up or persevere through the trials and tribulations that I was about to face.

Between 2007 and 2010, I had three major crises occur in my life. The first crisis was the death of my kidneys, the second was the death of my marriage, and the third was the death of my mother. Each one represented a life-altering moment. I was rocked to the core mentally, emotionally, and physically. Each crisis brought on a different set of issues. Nothing could have prepared me for what I was about to experience.

PHYSICAL CRISIS

In 2007, I was diagnosed with lupus nephritis, an autoimmune disease in which the body's immune system targets and attacks its own body tissues and organs. In my case, the organs affected the most were my kidneys. The results from my kidney biopsy revealed such severe inflammation of my kidneys that I was prescribed six months of chemotherapy treatments to suppress the lupus activity that was damaging them. The side effects of the chemotherapy were so severe that I had major hair loss, poor appetite, darkening of my skin and nails, diarrhea, swelling, and major joint pain. My kidney function continued to decline rapidly and I entered stage 4 renal failure; my kidneys were barely working at all. My doctors warned me that I would need dialysis if I was going to survive, for without it, my death was imminent.

MENTAL CRISIS

Emotionally, I was a wreck. My mental state had become unstable, for not only was I grieving the loss of my kidney, I was also grieving the loss of my marriage. In August 2007, my husband asked me for a divorce in the midst of my medical crisis. I became depressed and emotionally broken. I simply could not understand or comprehend why he had chosen that moment to ask me for a divorce. What was going through my mind was my wedding vows where he vowed to love me and support me "in sickness and in health until death do us part." By his action that vow was broken. Instead of being a shelter during the storm, he became the wolf who blew our house down. Reconciliation was nowhere in sight. Our separation became a major hindrance, and it destroyed the family peace and structure in our home. Suddenly, my financial status was in jeopardy, for I had no additional income outside of my unemployment income. The mental stress from dealing with each crisis was too hard to bear.

PARENTAL CRISIS

I had just arrived home from the airport after visiting my youngest daughter who was attending college in Houston, Texas. Upon arrival, I was immediately rushed to the hospital, for the doctor wanted to speak to me about my mother's diagnosis. For over six years, she had battled lung cancer. I was her caregiver; I was tasked with making sure she was able to get to every treatment. For four hours during each treatment session, I would sit and talk to my mother to make sure that she was comforted. While attending to my mother's care, I was still receiving my treatments that I needed relating to my chronic kidney disease diagnosis.

The stress of taking care of my mother and myself had begun to take a toll on my body. I had become ill and unable to care for my mother. My sibling was having a hard time dealing with the fact that our mother was dying and that the end was near. At the meeting, the doctor informed me that there was nothing else they could do and advised my mother to go on home hospice care immediately. The idea of losing my only parent who was active in my life was hard for me live with. Since I had been ten years old, I'd had to help my mother, and now I had to deal with losing her right at the point in my life that I needed her most.

On May 17, 2010, my mother was sent home from the hospital to hospice care and on June 6, 2010, she died. The death of my mother was a major blow. Five months later, following her death, I was admitted to the hospital for emergency surgery to start my dialysis treatment. Her death was my rock bottom and my sifting moment. In three short years, I lost my marriage, my mother, and my kidneys.

As Christians, we know we will experience many trials in our lives. The hardships that we go through are not designed to break us, but to strengthen us and refine our character as believers in Jesus Christ. In my dream, the Holy Spirit did not promise that I was not going to suffer, but I was given the assurance that I would recover and when I did, I would strengthen others in their hardships. Through my crisis, I learned that I had grit and I had what it takes to be an overcomer. Since my childhood, God had instilled in me a survival spirit. At an early age, I had to learn how to stand tall when adversity came my way. I learned that God uses our experiences for our good and not for our bad. He used the journey that I went through and also the path, the strategy, the plan that God had for me knowing at this time and this season how I was going to overcome it. My adversities were not meant to destroy me. They were meant to teach me and build me up and train me how to be that overcomer that God destined me to be. It was a plan that was set in motion by God so that I would come to that point to see that I was destined for greatness, even from the beginning.

The path set for me was not for me to skip past the journey, but my journey was to bring to life the word of God in the twenty-first century. God was molding me and shaping me to be His 21st century miracle. He was using me as His champion of war, a beacon of hope, and light for those who have been downtrodden and discouraged, and those who felt their life had no purpose.

From the beginning, God wanted me to learn that I not only had purpose, but that all that I went through, and am presently going through, was part of His original plan. He is giving me the strategies, tools, and weapons to help others to not only survive but thrive in this time and season. Just like he dealt with Paul on the Damascus Road, he had to show me what it was going to take for me to be able to go into the masses to encourage and inspire others and to be that living epistle for all to see. No one could see the scars that I was carrying on the inside when my husband asked me for a divorce after I became ill. Those scars ran deep inside my inner core, but on the outside all people would see was a smile. As women who are brokenhearted and hurt, we wear the scars of rejection and abandonment well. We wrongly believe that to show any sign of emotional hurt is showing a sign of shame. To live a life of transformation and change, we must be willing to be vulnerable and open to surrender to God's will allow Him to make us whole. God took my scars that I had hidden deep down in my heart and turned my misery into ministry.

CHAPTER 6

A Change Brings a Change

"Stepping onto a brand-new path is difficult, but not more difficult than remaining in a situation, which is not nurturing to the whole woman"

—*Maya Angelou*

I never saw myself as someone of value until I remembered the words that my high school counselor, Mr. Patterson, spoke into my life. He said that I am a leader, and I am an atmosphere changer. He said that one day I would come to a crossroad where I would have to decide if I was going to become a leader or a follower. That crossroad came in November 2010, when I was told by my physician that I would have to start dialysis. In the beginning I thought dialysis meant not only an upheaval, but the end of my life. I felt abandoned and alone. For three years, I experienced both the mental and medical challenges of adjusting to life with renal disease. When I would hear the words *dialysis* or *end stage renal failure*, all I could think of was that I was going to die, and my life was coming to an end. In my mind, starting dialysis was the beginning stage of my death; I was certain my life would be over soon.

A CHANGE HAS COME

Three days a week for four and a half hours each day, I was required to undergo dialysis treatments. The treatment process caused physical stress on my body. After each treatment, I would be so tired and weak that I could not spend adequate time caring for my children, grandchildren, or other family members. Because I felt mentally and physically drained all the time, participating in family outings or events became non-existent. Dialysis had begun to affect every area of my life to the point where I made up my mind not to comply with the prescribed treatment plan. I knew that the decision for non-compliance was essentially a death wish.

I was a person who believed that failure was not an option. With the loss of my marriage, my health, and my mother, I saw my life as a complete failure. I had no hope for the future, and I was in this battle alone. How untrue that really was! During one treatment at the dialysis clinic, I became distracted by the words of a patient sitting two seats down from me. I could hear her saying, "Lord, I don't want to do this anymore, please take my life now." You see, she was saying out loud the words that I was saying to myself internally. I wanted to die, for I did not believe that I had any value to bring to any relationship, whether it was with a male companion, my family, my friends, or God. Dialysis was affecting every area of my life. It was affecting my time, my treasure, and my talent. I had become a broken woman all over again. I was broken mentally and physically. I could not see the beauty of living anymore.

Before dialysis, I was known as a "radical of heart" and an atmosphere changer. I was the person that lived my life to the fullest in good times or bad. Nevertheless, the effects of starting dialysis and losing both my marriage and my mother in a short time span resulted in my going down a road of sorrow and despair all over again. I had given up on life and on everyone in my life. All I wanted to do was simply end the pain that I was experiencing and find peace in death. However, hearing the words of the other patient helped me to see past the negative self-talk and the destructive mindset. I felt my purpose being birthed inside of me. I gained a renewed strength and fervor; a fervor and desire to bring a change in my life and in the lives of others. At that moment, I gained the strength and ability to take my mind off myself and focus on someone else. As a very independent person, it was difficult accepting my illness, but once I realized that I was not alone and there were others who had experienced what I was going through and lived, I began to see a new focus and clear vision for my life. My vision was to empower people overcoming adversities such as chronic illness in their lives. I realized that living with renal failure does not mean the end of my life, but instead it was the beginning of new hope, a new beginning, and a new change in my life.

"A change brings a change" represents transformation, and thinking about transformation raises the question, "What are you going to do differently?" Are you going to keep doing the same thing or are you willing to make a change? Insanity is doing the same thing and expecting a different result. Implementing the new changes in my life allowed me to see the joy and purpose in everything that I have gone through. I realized that every day, people face battles and challenges that often rock their world. Some may even appear doomed to end in failure, but I have learned through all my negative experiences that all things are possible to overcome and that you are not alone. With God all things are possible. The adversities that I experienced did not mean the end for me; they were the beginning of a second chance—a second chance to live my life to the fullest and on my own terms.

SECOND CHANCES

Change is inevitable! We know that seasons change. It can be hot one minute and cold the next. We know that everybody's situation changes. We know that people change. One minute we are up and another minute we are down, and in some cases, we may seem crazy and out of our minds. However, the one good thing that I learned is that God never changes. According to Hebrews 13:8 (NIV), *"Jesus Christ is the same yesterday and today and forever."* Jesus remains the same in the past, present, and the future. It brings me comfort to know just as God never changes, God's word never changes, nor will it return void. God's word will accomplish everything that God intended to be carried out and God always keeps His promises.

As a Christian, I have been taught that God is a God of second chances—a second chance at life and a second chance at abundance. When I was first diagnosed with a chronic illness, I believed that my life was over. I believed everything that I desired to achieve in life had become unattainable and unachievable. I could not see past the hurt, the shame, and the pain from everything that I had been going through until God changed my heart and my mindset. Proverbs 23:7 (NKJV) says, *"For as he thinks in his heart, so is he."* The Bible teaches us that the issues of life flow from your heart. Although your heart is internal, what is in your heart will have a direct impact on what you are thinking. For what you believe in your heart, you will manifest.

The rejection by my husband and my parents had a direct impact on how I acted and how I was thinking about myself and life in general. I could not see a future, for my current life was so filled with one negative situation and circumstance after another. I could not think clearly, nor could I see clearly. In my heart, I had made up in my mind that everything that I was experiencing was my fault and I deserved it. I was an accident, and I should never had been born. The outcomes in my relationships were warranted, for I did not deserve love, nor did I know what true love really is.

My mind was cluttered with so many negative things from my past and my present. My divorce was the trigger that forced me to deal with my true emotions and my true feelings that I had locked away deep down in my heart. I had locked the hurt and the pain so deep down in my heart that my life was a pretense. I realized that until I dealt with my true inner being and emotions, I would forever continue the cycle of sorrow that I had created for myself.

PART THREE

THE BIRTH OF PURPOSE AND IDENTITY

CHAPTER 7

Renew Your Mind

"Don't copy the behavior and customs of this world, but let God transform you into a new person by changing the way you think…"
—**Romans 12:2 (NLT)**

For years, I have heard the term "You are what you think." English philosopher James Allen wrote, "As a man thinks, so he is; as he continues to think, so he remains." Author Earl Nightingale wrote, "We become what we think about." In the Bible, Proverbs 23:7 (NKJV) says, *"For as he thinks in his heart, so is he…."*. As I consider these three phrases, they can be summarized: It is our thoughts that create our experiences, we become what we think, and the thoughts we allow in our mind shape our daily life and determine our future.

One of the greatest lessons that I've learned was that my life will not change for the better until I make up my mind to do better. For as long as I can remember, I faced the hardship of living in lack. The lack of joy in my life, the lack of peace in my mind, and the lack of financial stability. No matter how much success I had achieved in those areas, I still fell short. The truth behind it all was that I was not mentally fit. Although I was a high-achieving and high-functioning person, I was mentally unstable. Being mentally stable requires you to have the ability to deal with past and present traumas that appear in your life; unfortunately, I did not have that ability. Each day, I found myself seeking the answer to one question: "Why?" *Why did God allow these things to happen to me? Why did my mother not love me? Why did my father reject me? Why did my husband leave me? Why can't I find someone to love me for me and take care of me?*

My divorce triggered negative emotions and anxious thoughts I believed I had overcome many years ago. Since my childhood, I have dealt with the emotional trauma of rejection and abandonment from my mother and father. The anxiety of not knowing what my future would bring for me, either spiritually or financially, was very frustrating and frightening. The stress of the separation was too great to deal with. The idea of having to start over triggered my emotions of feeling lonely and abandoned all over again. In addition, there was the guilt and shame of getting a divorce as a Christian woman. The "If I…" phrase overwhelmed my thoughts and my emotions. I would say to myself, *If I would have only prayed more, if I would have fasted more, if I would have loved him more, or if I would have catered to him more, would that have been enough to get him to stay?* As I looked back, I realized that I had lost myself to the idea of being married and my identity was defined by being a married woman. So, when I became a divorced woman, I lost my self-worth, my value, and my identity. I did not know who I really was or who I would become.

For several months, I was lost and depressed. I had no desire to live or move forward in my life. In the daytime, I would smile and act like everything was okay, but at night, I would cry in despair. The stress of dealing with my true feelings began to affect my health; it showed up in my body, as the symptoms from chronic high blood pressure complications began to affect my kidneys and my heart. It wasn't long before my mental issues showed themselves in my behavior, which affected my relationships with my family and friends.

It was at that point that I realized I needed to acknowledge my pain and my hurt and I began to deal with the emotions that I had suppressed. I discovered that dealing with my emotions and my true feelings is the only way to overcome my past and present hurts and start the journey of living my life authentically to rediscover my purpose and identity. I learned that developing a new mindset, a growth mindset, is a critical step to having a healthy and empowering life.

A NEW MINDSET

I was inspired by God to read a book by Pastor Casey Treat called *Renewing the Mind: The Key to Transformation*. In his book, Pastor Casey states that "most people need and want real change in their life but feel it is impossible to attain." Throughout the book, he provides biblical truths that empowered me and taught me how to change my thinking, grow stronger spiritually, develop and understand my purpose, and maximize my potential. As I applied those truths in my life, I no longer had a defeatist mindset.

I began to move forward and experience God's plan and will for my life like never before. I began to focus on rebuilding myself from the inside out rather than from the outside in. No longer would I allow negative thoughts and actions to hinder me from reaching my full potential. I decided to take a journey on discovering my destiny and my identity and move beyond just surviving to thriving in all areas of my life, especially in the areas of my health, mindset, faith, relationships, and finances.

Romans 12:2 (NLT) says, ***"Don't copy the behavior and customs of this world, but let God transform you into a new person by changing the way you think."*** Simply put, you need to renew your mind by replacing your old way of thinking with the biblical truths taught in the word of God. Renewing your mind requires you to change your vision. In the book *Hello, Tomorrow!*, Dr. Cindy Trimm states, "Vision calls you out of your past into your future." Envisioning a better future for myself is what helped me to move forward toward reclaiming my life and all that I had had lost from childhood and after my divorce. Everything that I had desired to become was centered around the idea of being married, having children, securing a good job, and keeping my faith in God. However, when I lost my marriage, my vision was severed, and my identity was shattered into little broken pieces that were unrepairable.

Changing my thinking helped me to let go of past thoughts and past hurts so that I could become an active participant in developing my future. It pointed me toward transformation in knowing who I am and who I am becoming as a strong Black Christian woman, now divorced. Renewing my mind helped me to challenge my cultural norms and spiritual understanding. The most important step in renewing the mind is mastering thoughts.

When we are unhappy, we seek to create change. God's kingdom runs on faith, but the world's system runs on fear. A transformed mindset comes when you cease being afraid of the unknown and move forward into what is yet to come. It is the moment where your future becomes brighter than your past. It is the moment when hope abounds. A renewed mind focuses on the possibilities and opportunities and not past failures. For me to see past the pain and hurt that I experienced from parental rejection, spousal abandonment, and chronic mental and physical health issues, I had to be determined to develop a recovery plan for reclaiming my life, building up my self-worth and confidence, and planning my future.

CHAPTER 8

Faith Walk
Not Just a Faith Talk

When you decide to walk by faith, you don't get rid of trials. You learn to overcome them
—**Kenneth Copeland**

Faith is believing with the heart, your innermost being. Merriam-Webster defines *faith* as belief and trust in and loyalty to God. The biblical meaning of the word *faith* is confidence and trust. The object of our faith is God and His promises. Since experiencing major losses, my faith in God and His promises has been the foundation for overcoming the many adversities in my life.

Over the last ten years, my journey has been solely based on my trust in God and the purpose He has for my life. Second Corinthians 5:7 says, **"For we live by believing** *and not by seeing" (NLT).* There is a quote from Martin Luther King Jr. that says, "Faith is taking the first step, even when you don't see the whole staircase." Taking my first step towards healing, emotionally and physically, was the beginning of transformation in my life. Living by my motto, "A change brings a change," was the first step of trusting God and moving forward. It was the beginning process of living an abundant life.

FAITH OVER FEAR

Second Timothy 1:7 (NKJV) says, *"For God has not given us the spirit of fear, but of power, and of love and a sound mind."* Past trauma and negative outcomes have caused me to become afraid of what is possible. My lack of identity caused me to only see what other people saw in me and not what I saw in myself. Having the wrong images in my mind bound me and kept me from seeking and elevating to the level next. I realized that if you have no real identity then your purpose is unknown. Knowing neither who I was nor my purpose hindered me from operating in power and authority given unto me by God. I learned that negative and fearful thinking produce negative outcomes. This became the behavior pattern: I was operating in fear rather than fearlessness.

Research has shown that culture can influence our communication with other people, and it affects our values; what we consider right or wrong. The negative culture that

I grew up in helped shaped the bad habits and practices that caused negative outcomes in my life. Those outcomes became extremely painful and depressing. However, it was important for me to learn and understand that my situation does not determine my outcome. I learned that my past childhood trauma, my divorce, and my current health challenges do not determine my future. Those adversities that happened in my life cannot be changed, altered, or forgotten. So I learned to accept them, forgive, and move on. To maximize my full potential, I had to believe that I could do whatever I set out to do. Developing a renewed mindset was the tool that helped me to place faith over fear.

CHANGE YOUR HABITS

Walking by faith and not by sight changes the way we live. We are no longer bound by a finite mindset. A finite mindset consists of limited thinking and understanding of life. We are bound to the basic concept of things that we see, feel or touch. However, walking by faith opens our spiritual being to Godly insight and Godly wisdom. Our perspective in life as believers is to trust in God and his ability to bring us through whatever situation that we are facing. For three months, I had to overcome issues related to my health, mindset, faith, relationships, and my finances. The support system that I once had was now nonexistent. The life that I once lived was in jeopardy and I was all alone. Simply put, I was afraid!

Hebrews 11:1 says, *"Now faith is confidence in what we hope for and assurance about what we do not see"(NIV)*. This faith is true faith that consists of confidence, hope, and assurance in God and his ability to bring you out of your trouble and make a way out of no way. If I was going to move forward to my next level, I needed to have faith in God and believe that He will keep his promises. It is easy to trust in the tangible things, but as believers of Jesus Christ you must be courageous and learn to act according to the will of God.

It is easy to give up and continue to struggle mentally, emotionally, and financially. When I became divorced, uncertainty and trepidation filled my life. I was emotionally unstable, my faith was shaken, my health issues increased, and my financial struggles increased three-fold. It was then that I came across a passage in the Bible stating, **"For our present troubles are small and won't last very long. Yet they produce for us a glory that vastly outweighs them and will last forever" 2 Corinthians 4:17 (NLT)**. What this passage was saying to me is that trouble may come, but it will not last.

Although things seem hard now, in time, I will heal, and I will succeed if I just believe. For what is coming will be greater than what has been. At that very moment, I made up my mind that my struggles would not define my reality. I was determined to overcome my adversity and live a life in which I am the victor and not the victim.

To walk in my victory, I posted daily affirmations in the main rooms of my house. Words have power and my daily affirmations, or mantras, helped reprogram my thinking and boost my faith in God and His promises written in the Bible. Isaiah 55:11 says, ***"So shall My word be that goes forth from My mouth; It shall not return to Me void, but it shall accomplish what I please, and it shall prosper in the thing for which I sent it"*** (NKJV).

Throughout my life I believed in the words of individuals closest to me and the individuals whom I trusted the most. As a child, I believed in the words spoken to me by my parents, my friends, and my teachers. If they said I would never amount to anything, then I would believe it. My identity was shaped by what people said and what they thought of me. Over the years, I learned that unless I began to trust in my abilities in bringing change in my life, I would continue to remain stuck and live a mediocre life. Nevertheless, when I began to focus on my own goals and replace the negative thinking and negative self-talk with the biblical truths outlined in the word of God, not only did my outcome change, but my actions changed.

No longer was it a faith *talk*—it became a faith *walk*. Changing my habits and focusing on Christ changed my life. I began to understand God's mercy and love for me; it became the reason for transforming my life and my habits. By spending time in prayer, reading the scriptures and listening to the voice of God, I discovered my purpose and created a life where I am beginning to live my life victorious and empowered

Here are 7 specific habits to use to help transform your mindset and shape your life today:

1. Learn to exercise the skill of meditation.
2. Change your negative self-talk to an empowerment speech.
3. Surround yourself with positive people.
4. Create a long-term goal for yourself.
5. Adopt a healthy lifestyle. A healthy body will support a healthy mind.
6. Celebrate your mini wins!
7. Believe in the promises of God.

CHAPTER 9

You Can L.Y.V.E (Living Your Life Victorious and Empowered)

Life is not about how you survive the storm, but rather how you dance in the rain
—*Regina Brett*

My life journey started off yearning for the American dream: marriage, children, and a good job. However, my life's journey did not end up that way. My life started out with a lot of adversities, a lot of ups and downs. Because of all the hurt and the pain, I could not see the end; the possibility of living the good life was nowhere in sight. I was ten years old when I lost my American dream. My mother's grief, brought on by the death of my sister at an early age, was the jumpstart of a whirlwind of unfortunate events in my life, namely, parental abandonment and rejection, attempted suicide at the age of 15, bankruptcy at the age of 25, diagnoses of lupus and kidney failure, divorce, and emotional trauma due to losing my mother and starting dialysis in the same year. It's easy to give up when so many bad things happen to you. Nevertheless, I had to learn, as the oldest of four siblings, how to overcome pain and hurt in order to be a support and help for others rather than focusing on myself.

You see, the life that I knew and lived was full of trauma and chaos. Everything that surrounded me was nothing but darkness; it was hard to see the light of hope at the end of the tunnel. However, despite all my adversities, I overcame and I survived.

EXPECT THE UNEXPECTED

The Bible says in Jeremiah 1:5 (NLT), *"I knew you before I formed you in your mother's womb. Before you were born, I set you apart and appointed you as my prophet to the nations."* My journey of self-discovery and identity began when I started to search for a true understanding of God's will in my life. I learned that everything that I endured throughout my childhood and adult life was part of my journey of self-discovery. From my childhood, I based my identity on approval from other people, but I quickly learned that in order to become the person who

God called me to be, I had to begin to believe in myself. I learned that I have the power within me to change my outcome, and the power to overcome any adversities that try to overtake me.

Living your life victorious and empowered requires you to become the architect of your life. Only you can choose how to live it. Everything depends on your actions and the decisions that you make for yourself. Otherwise, anybody can come and define your identity and your self-worth. In my case, that is exactly what happened. You see, the shock and the betrayal of my divorce, along with numerous health and mental issues, caused me to feel so unworthy that I wanted to die. The thought of taking my life was the trigger that caused me to pause and start doing some self-reflection as to what was really going on with me and my true feelings and emotions. I started to access my true heart. I began to see that I had purpose; I was chosen by God and saved for a reason. It's because of that discovery that I began to turn my life around. I sought to live my life on purpose and began to live my life to the fullest.

The key point is when you discover your self-worth and learn to maximize your full potential in your life; that's when you're able to overcome any adversity and become resilient. You have been given the power by God to be an overcomer and to thrive and not just survive. God has called you a champion and he is shaping you in his image, perfect in every way. You see, once I discovered my identity and purpose, my focus and pursuit were to change my thinking and rid my life of negative thoughts and toxic influences.

For me to live a life of transformation and change, I had to be willing to be vulnerable and open to surrender to God's will and allow Him to make me whole. It is God who formed our inner part and shaped us in His image. Overcoming rejection and deep hurt through my journey of forgiveness opened the doors for me for empowerment, opportunity, and growth in every area of my life. I learned to expect the unexpected. It's because of the transformation in my life that I can live my best life in spite of any obstacles that might come my way. No longer am I living my life in fear and hopelessness. I am now living my life victorious and empowered.

ENDNOTES

CHAPTER 7

Treat, C. (1992) Renewing the Mind: The Key to Transformation. Harrison House. Tulsa, Oklahoma.

Trimm, C. (2018) Hello, Tomorrow! Charisma House. Lake Mary, Florida.

www.ingramcontent.com/pod-product-compliance
Lightning Source LLC
Chambersburg PA
CBHW060503110426
42738CB00055B/2605